BOO BOO and the GENERAL

BOO BOO and the GENERAL

NICHOLAS APOSTOL

PRIMIX
PUBLISHING
THE WRITE CHOICE

Primix Publishing
East Brunswick Office Evolution
1 Tower Center Boulevard, Ste 1510
East Brunswick, NJ 08816
www.primixpublishing.com
Phone: 1-800-538-5788

Original Manuscript, layout, design
By Nicholas Apostol

Excerpts from Memoir of Mary Hall Caine
Reproduced by permission of
Nicholas Apostol

Cover design
by Nicholas Apostol

All photographs and illustrations from originals contained in scrapbook prepared by Frank A. Armstrong and Mary Hall Caine now exclusive property of Nicholas Apostol

Published by Primix Publishing: 04/15/2025

ISBN: 979-8-89194-453-4(sc)
ISBN: 979-8-89194-454-1(e)

Library of Congress Control Number: 2025905411

Contents

Author's Note ix

Introduction 1

Epilogue 59

About the Author 63

Dedicated to
Boo-Boo, Army
and all the men and women to
whom we owe so much and
knew so little about.

Author's Note

Love and war are unique attributes of the human species. It is quite remarkable that they can coexist being one the antithesis of the other.

The first may be the single greatest achievement of the human spirit while war may be its most abject failure.

The story of Boo-Boo and the General is a modern day Shakespearian tragedy to equal Romeo and Juliette. It highlights their very human frailties that were kept very private if not a secret between themselves for years. It is told in their own words and I have woven within them artifacts from those times - the only side that the public and even their own closest family members would have seen.

The purpose was not to explain their own marital failures or successes but rather to highlight the triumph of their love for each other. Though in every respect these two disparate spirits enjoyed a most successful lifetime by all measurements of such, their inability to fully realize a life together was their very own tragedy.

Their love endured despite the knowledge that they could never be together. Both placed duty above their own selfish desire – he to his career and she to her children. There is no doubt whatsoever their love for each other was genuine and they silently took that love to their graves notwithstanding the pain it caused them.

I had the privilege of personally knowing many of the players in this romantic tragedy and will be a better person for that. The story is told so others who may suffer the same fate will know their path has already been trodden. It is meant as a record for the ages and in no way meant to be judgmental.

It is worthy of note that the General kept a diary and numerous scrapbooks throughout his career. With the exception of the scrapbook for his two years in England which belongs to the Author, the remainder can be reviewed at the East Carolina University. Though they provide a keen insight into the General's professional career, there is little relating to his personal side.

Boo-Boo on the other hand was a very private person, keeping her feelings to herself. She did not document nor communicate much about her life until I gave her a computer in her 75th year and insisted she learn to use it and write down her memories. From those recollections emerged the story now told in the pages to follow.

If you can't be with the one you love,
Then love the one you're with…..

Stephen Stills

Introduction

War represents human nature at its worst. Both cowardice and heroism can co-exist and for the most part man's worst characteristics must dominate in order to survive.

Love on the other hand is the very antithesis of war. It brings out the best in mankind and seeks to touch the very essence of life often resulting in the creation of life itself.

That war and love can co-exist and even flourish simultaneoulsly is a tribute to the complexity of mankind. And so it was that in the darkest hours of World War II just such a seeming contradiction occurred when a 39 year old battle hardened American soldier met an aristocratic 25 year old English girl at RAF Polebrook in January 1942.

During the ensuing months the two found the meaning of true love but due to their circumstances would be unable to remain together. Both were in unhappy marriages and both had a child to care for. The war that brought them together would eventually force them apart and it would be more than 10 long years before they would realize the tragedy of their circumstances had denied them the ability to enjoy their love together, forever.

He was the gallant General Frank A. Armstrong Jr. who led the 8th Air Force in the first bombing raids over Germany. His role was made famous in a book called "Twelve O'Clock High" and later in a film of the same name starring Gregory Peck.

He had joined the U.S. Army Air Corps and had been nicknamed "Army" being short for "Armstrong". He was a half Cherokee North Carolina native born in 1902. He married in 1929 in Virginia and he nicknamed his wife "fluffy" though he mentions very little of her thereafter. It was said that he began procedures to divorce her for infidelity but stopped when he was informed that she was pregnant with his only son, Frank Armstrong III, in 1930. After an illustrious career and reaching the rank of Lieutenant General in the US Air Force, Frank Jr. retired in August 1962 after 6 years as Commander of the Alaskan Joint Command. His wife, Fluffy, died in 1962 as well. He returned to North Carolina and died in 1969. His son was shot down and killed over Laos in the Vietnam War in 1967. His remains have never been recovered.

She was Mary Hall Caine, daughter of a prominent British industrialist and Member of Parliament and granddaughter of Sir Thomas Hall Caine, one of England's most famous authors. She was an officer in the American Red Cross and was assigned to the American airmen stationed at RAF Polebrook, home to the 97th Heavy Bombardment Group. The men nicknamed her "Boo Boo" because of the way she would purse her lips when disappointed or unhappy. She had two children and moved to the US in 1955 after divorcing her first husband. She met up again with Frank in the US and after three years, she remarried a pre-war friend though for practical reasons – not love. Her eldest son, Michael, graduated from the Citadel Military Academy in the early 1960s as an officer in the US Army. Her youngest son, Nicholas, was an Airman in the U.S. Air Force during the Vietnam conflict earning a Commendation Medal for his services. After her second husband died she moved to Stuart, Florida where she died in 2003. Both her sons still live in the Stuart area.

Together Boo-Boo and the General had found the meaning of life and love which they had failed to find with anyone else. Though they knew their love for each other was doomed from the start, the march of death all around them kept them living for the moment and oblivious to what the future might bring.

During those two short years in England, they created a scrapbook and Frank kept it up until many years later. He shared his every promotion from Colonel to two star General with his true love and gave her some of those mementos like his gold ID bracelet bearing his first star and inscribed with his nickname, a brace of stars for his collar when he was promoted to Major General, some campaign ribbons and awards as well as his command pilot wings he wore over enemy lines and during much of his career.

The following pages include the pictures, news clippings, letters and other memorabilia from the scrapbook they shared together as well as some exerpts from Boo-Boo's diary and autobiography.

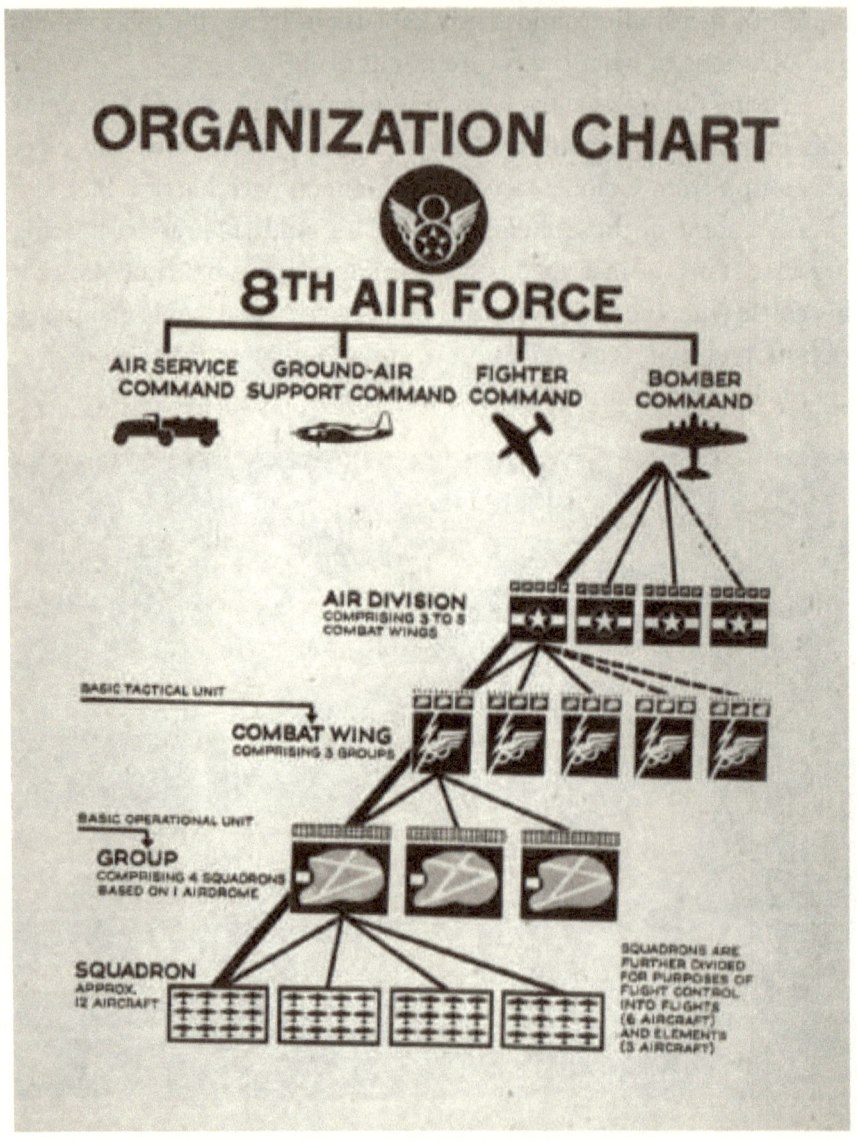

Armstrong started as a Lt. Colonel on January 5th, 1942 as Chief of Operations for the new Bomber Command and then became a Colonel on March 1st commanding the 97th Bomber Group. On February 8th, 1943 he was promoted to Brigadier General taking command of the 1st Combat Wing in June and then became Division Commander. General Ira Eaker was the Bomber Command commanding general.

In January 1942, now Lt. Col. Armstrong (front row), was chosen by Brigadier General Eaker to create the VIIIth Bomber Command which would later become the 8th Air Force

In July 1942, Armstrong took over the 97th Bomber Group and was promoted to full Colonel. This picture remained next to Boo-Boo's bedside for most of the rest of her life.

This portrait was taken by TIME-LIFE's famous photographer Margaret Bourke-White in London. Frank Armstrong gave it to Boo-Boo to mark his promotion to Colonel. He inscribed the original copy with: *"Booboo"*

> *Yes he wears a*
> *pair of "silver*
> *wings" just for you.*
> *Polebrook   Frank Armstrong*
> *Col. A.A.F.*
> *4/24/42*

Excerpts from Boo-Boo's memoires continue)

In 1942 the Americans came into the war and when we set out one morning Marion said:
"Dearie, my guys are in it too now so we will go to the 8th army air

corps headquarters where they have taken over the girl's school in High Wycombe which is part of my territory and I want to see if there is something I can do for them. But dearie, you be careful - you are not to fall in love with one of those boys. Americans can be very attractive you know!"

"Not to worry" I replied. "I will never fall in love again. As far as I am concerned all men are the same and love is for the birds!" With that I turned the car towards High Wycombe and the next chapter of my life.

The girl's school was a beautiful old, stone manor house with lovely grounds, a lake and acres of lawns. We drove up the driveway and saw a few officers hurrying around in their uniforms of pink trousers and olive green jackets. One came over to see what we wanted and Marion said she had come to see the commanding officer who turned out to be General Eaker.

We waited a short time in the large hall and then were ushered in to a room with nothing in it but a large desk. The General rose and explained that they were far from settled in, which was obvious, and then he called a young officer.

"Do you think you could rustle up a couple of chairs for these ladies?"

"Yes sir" and a few minutes later we were given a chair each. Marion told him since they were countrymen of hers she wondered if there was something she could do for them. They talked away and she explained what she did. His face lit up and he told us that he would love to have us take care of his boys as he did not like the American Red Cross and would not deal with them. She explained that our organization was far too small to be able to cope with the needs of the 8th Army Air corps!!

He finally agreed that we should join the American Red Cross and he would deal exclusively with us. She was already in the ATS so he decided to make me an officer in the Army Air Corps. That way he would only have to deal with Marion and me as her assistant. He had some cloth brought to him which he handed over to me to have sewn into a pink skirt and the olive green for a jacket.

Suddenly everything was very busy and it seemed there were only officers as the enlisted guys had not yet arrived. Only the top brass was available to set everything up. He told us he wanted to give a party to meet the Mayor of the town and all the local gentry so that they would be accepted in the community. Marion was perfect for that as she knew everyone. So she said she would take care of that. After more discussions about the party he intimated that they would need to decorate the main hall. Marion decided that this would be my job! He called to one of the passing officers to ask Major Armstrong to come in. I heard a deep voice say:

"Sir, you sent for me?"

"Yes, I want you to meet Lady Chesham, and this young lady who is her assistant. Please show the young lady around and help her with anything she might want. They will be in charge of the party for our neighbors"

I looked up into the most piercing eyes. He was well tanned and grey haired and those piercing eyes had a strange twinkle in them. We went out and he showed me the Great Hall which was quite impressive and I wondered how on earth I would decorate it. I asked him if the garden had any flowers. He told me he did not know as they had been so busy since they had arrived that he had not had a chance to look around. We both *laughed and sauntered outside into the garden. We came upon a whole area filled with Magnolia trees.*

"You know this would be great. I could make it all Magnolias but how to cut them and get them up in the Hall?"

He said not to worry he would take care of it.

"Can you really?" I spluttered. "That would be wonderful. I will check on when the party is to take place and be back. Thank you so much for your help"

He smiled. It was almost a boyish grin and said:"I haven't done anything yet!"

After receiving the Distinguished Flying Cross, he sent this picture along with the ribbon to Boo-Boo and on the picture inscribed:*"Just to Frighten you – Frank".* Boo-Boo wrote on the back of the photograph: *"It did – Boo".* Then she folded it up and sent it back (hence the creases in the photograph). When she later put it in the scrap book page she wrote: *"Scared !"*.

Boo-Boo joined the Red Cross in 1941 and in early 1942 found herself assigned to the recently arrived American detachment with headquarters in High Wycombe in northeast London.

It was there that she met the dashing Lt. Colonel Armstrong. Among other famous people she would befriend at that base in the ensuing two years would include such notables as James H. Doolittle, the aviator and later four star general remembered in the book and film "30 seconds over Tokyo".

Some famous Hollywood actors would also serve their country as Air Force reservists. These included Lieutenant James "Jimmy" Stewart, Lieutenant Clark Gable and Lieutenant Gene Raymond. All flew missions on B-17s and were highly decorated for their bravery. Stewart retired as Brigadier General in the 1960s. Though they all knew Boo-Boo well they also knew that she was Army's girl.

Armstrong had even penned a song to be sung to the tune of "Camptown Races" which went like this:

"The US Air Corps sings this song
Boo Boo, Boo Boo
But Colonel Army's so big and strong,
He sings Boo Boo all day;
They're goin' to dance all night,
they're goin' to sleep all day,
I'll bet my money Army's the lad
that Booboo loves today."

We went back to join Marion and the General and soon we were on our way. I was very attracted to his accent which Marion told me was southern because he came from the hills of North Carolina. Later I would learn he was half Cherokee Indian.

The next weeks were taken up with getting our uniforms made and joining the American Red Cross which never asked about my passport. All went very smoothly. We got the invitations out for the party and on the day it was to take place I went over to decorate the big Hall. I did not have to wonder long on how I would handle it. Major Armstrong came out and had the boys cutting down the branches of Magnolias. He himself was up a tree much to the amusement of the enlisted boys. It was all brought in to the Hall and I was up the ladder much to his concern. We managed to get the whole room decorated amidst a lot of laughter. When I left, he said:

"I will see you tonight, you are coming?" I said I would be there but late as I had another party I had promised to go to that night with an English officer. He said:

"I will wait by the door for you so please do not disappoint me." That voice could charm the devil himself and it did have quite an effect on me.

I had forgotten all about the British cocktail party but felt I had to go so I was quite late getting to the 8th Air Force party. When I did get there, he was by the door as promised and Marion scolded me for being so late. She told me that the Major had never left the door and was so worried I was not going to turn up.

She said: "He is crazy about you, but do not forget what I told you, dearie." Later that night when we left he came over to my car and asked me if I would go with him and a friend, a Colonel, and his friend to her house for a drink. She was waiting in her car and apparently she lived close by, so I agreed and the four of us took off.

Major Armstrong was known as Army. He decided to call me Boo-Boo due to a pout I made pushing my lower lip out when things did not go as planned. We arrived at Barbara's house in about fifteen minutes; there was no one home and Army told me her husband was in the forces. Barbara settled us with drinks and then took the Colonel's hand and led him to her bedroom and said to us: "just make yourselves at home – the guest room is right there", waving her hand in the direction of another door. I was shocked and horrified and must have shown it as Army said; "Boo, you do not have to do anything you do not want to, please just sit down here beside me and we can talk."

It turned out Army was taken completely by surprise. He told me we would never go out with any of these characters again. He was very annoyed and it certainly nearly ended everything right then and there for me. As it was, we talked quietly getting to know each other and then the other two emerged, amazed to find us still sitting there just chatting. We went out to the car and told Barbara we had to get back. When Army saw me into my car he apologized profusely and I could tell he had not been a party to what had happened. He said he would see me the next day as we were due to go up to the base he would be in command of.

We saw more and more of each other but I kept it platonic, I was not ready for anything else and he respected my feelings. We had not talked *of our private lives. I had said I wanted to keep it that way. As our love grew for each other I said I would like to keep this as something carved out of space. I want to keep this as just another experience and I did not intend to fall in love.*

It proved easier said than done, but I had never been to bed with any man but my husband and that had not been a very happy experience. I was not keen to take the final step but it was not possible to keep our relationship platonic much longer. I knew I was very attracted to him and with a war raging time was not on our side.

I wrote to Andy saying I had fallen for another man and what were his intentions. It was so long since I had heard from him? Did he intend to come back to be my husband again or could he care less? I finally received a letter from him in which he never answered my question. I knew he had received my letter as he answered other questions, so I decided he did not care and I should do whatever seemed right for me.

Army had been promoted to Colonel and we went out to celebrate before returning to the Chesham's house where I was presently living. We chatted for a while with John and Marion then they went up to their room. They both adored Army and just told me not to stay up late as we had an early start the next morning.

We sat on the floor in front of a lovely fire and talked for a while. He still did not know I was married and I knew nothing of his home life and that was the way I wanted to keep it. His mouth became more demanding and it was there in front of the fire that we made love the first time. It seemed as though the universe exploded and then total peace. This I thought was the way it should be though it had never been that way with Andy. He was incredibly gentle for being such a strong man. I was lost but refused to believe it. He saw me to my room and then was gone. His driver was waiting in the driveway and I listened to the car leave and the sound of the crunching of the gravel that I would soon get to know well.

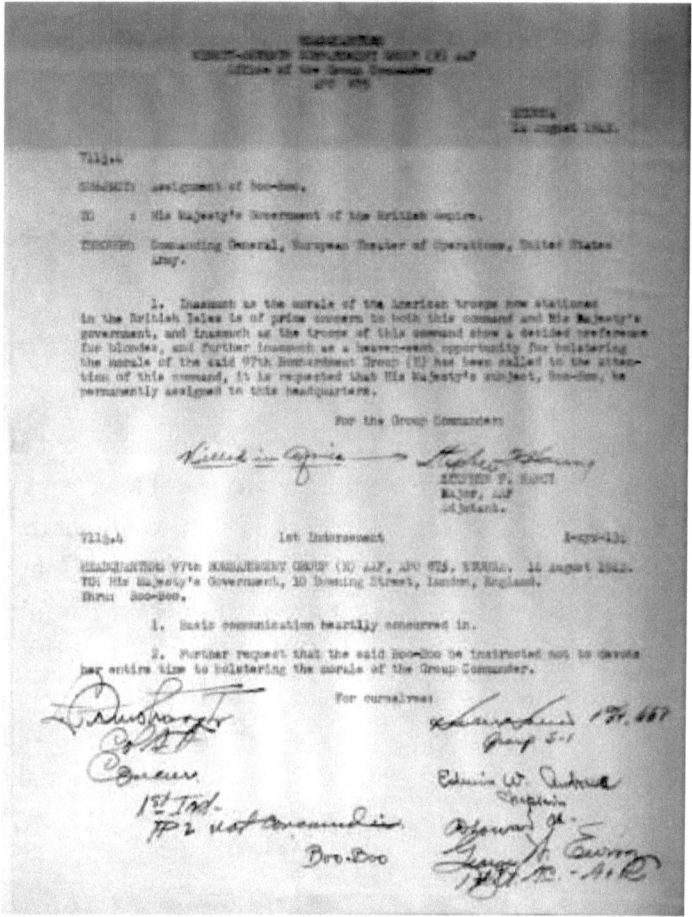

Boo-Boo was so popular that a fictional set of orders were issued requesting her permanent assignment signed by the Adjutant and endorsed by Armstrong and staff who asked that she not devote *"all her attention to Armstrong"*. She concurred with paragraph 1 but did not concur with paragraph 2 and signed herself as *"Boo-Boo"*. These moments of fun helped keep everyone's mind off the business of war.

On August 17th, 1942, Col. Frank A. Armstrong climbed into the co-pilot's seat of a B-17E serial number 41-2578 named *"Butcher Shop"* and with Pilot-in-Command Captain Paul W. Tibbetts took off on the first USAAF strategic bombing mission over enemy territory in Europe.

At the time, Frank had not been checked out and rated as Pilot-in-Command of the B-17 so had to fly right seat. However, as senior officer he gained the credit as the leader and commander of the flight. Tibbetts would later gain fame in the Pacific as pilot and Commander of the "Enola Gay" – the B-29 that dropped the first Atomic bomb on Japan to end the war. Armstrong also wound up in the Pacific Theater of Operations and having led the first strategic bombing by USAAF forces in Europe, he had the distinction of leading the last strategic bombing run of the war dropping conventional bombs from a B-29 over Japan exactly three years to the day later on August 15th, 1945.

RAF Polebrook and a B-17G overhead

The 97ᵗʰ Bomber Group heads out on a
Mission to bomb Germany.

"The whole show went off as planned... I saw the bombs hit the target... they were clustered closely together and I could see dirt and smoke flying into the air."

That is what Brigadier-general Ira C. Eaker, Commanding-general United States Army Air Force Bomber Command, said after yesterday's raid by United States bombers on Rouen. Here he is climbing out of the Flying Fortress in which he led the raid.

Brigadier General Ira C. Eaker, commanding general of the 8th Air Force Bomber Command rode along as an observer in a second Group of bombers that followed Col. Armstrong and Captain Tibbetts during the first daylight strategic bomb run over enemy territory on August 17, 1942.

Armstrong, Margaret Bourke-White and Actor Gene Raymond in 1942

Frank Armstrong was equally popular among the troops. Boo-Boo referred to him as a "man's man" because the airmen under his command were treated with great respect and they felt as if he were one of them.

Col. Armstrong, a right guy to his crew.

Loading up the Fortress with .50 calibre stuff. Crouching in front is Sgt. Alvin Horning, Mifflington, Pa.; standing (left to right) are: Sgt. Frank Rebello, Tiverton, R. I.; Sgt. Joseph F. Cummings, Oskaloosa, Ia.; Sgt. Dick Williams, Unadilla Forks, N. Y.; Sgt. Rudolph Turansky (other picture at right), New York City; Sgt. Chester C. Love, Cincinnati, and Sgt. Zane Gemmill, St. Clair, Pa.

Next morning I was driving up to the base where we had work to do and I guess I was very silent. Marion told me to keep my eyes on the road. I was as usual looking up trying to count the planes coming in from an early morning raid. That is about the way things were from then on. Army led all the first bombing flights over France and later Germany. We lived for the moment. One could not think beyond that as there might not be a beyond and that was unthinkable.

Army was no longer going on missions over enemy territory because he was too valuable to the Air Corps. He had been promoted once again and was now a Brigadier General. He was annoyed being tied to a desk and would escape to lead a group whenever possible. He told me that he did not like being a "Fuddy Duddy" as he called it!

I was given a new assignment which took me to Liverpool. I was to drive a man from the State Department who was some important official who wanted to see first- hand what we had been doing there for the war effort. So I took him around the Red Cross facilities in the area and we worked well together. He was very nice and fun to be with and seemed to find me amusing too. All went well until one day he said to me that it seemed kind of silly for me to sit at one table for my meals while he sat at another one in the same dining room. I agreed to move to his table. We talked of just about everything and he was drawing me out and eventually asked about the General. I was surprised he knew and so I said as little as possible. I should have seen the light but I did not. Then one evening he asked me to go over some papers with him and the map of England. It was after dinner so he suggested we spread it all out in his room – quickly adding that he had a private sitting room for the purpose of receiving guests.

Once there I realized it was trouble. As soon as we had everything laid out on the floor, he started coming on to me and I had to pretty well fight him off. When he realized I was going to make a scene and cause trouble for him, he let me go saying: "why am I different to the General?"

I told him I was in love with the General which was a different matter. I left and in the morning when I looked for him, the hotel told me he had left early that morning for London. I knew then that trouble was coming but thought he would incriminate himself if he complained about me.

I left too and on the way back stopped off at the base where Army was stationed. He was in a meeting when I got there but Gene Raymond greeted me and took me in to the Mess for lunch. Gene said the General would join us as soon as he was finished. We had just started when I felt faint and whispered to Gene to get me out of there as I did not want to collapse in the Mess. He was so sweet and he and another officer assisted me back to the General's quarters and called the doctor. I had done too much and was in a nervous state so he gave me something to calm me and had me stay lying down on Army's bed where I drifted off to sleep.

I awoke to Army saying "Honey, did you come back to me just to die?" I opened my eyes and smiled. Just hearing his voice did me so much good.

The next day I proceeded to London and when I called Marion she told me all hell was going on at Red Cross HQ where this horrid State Department man had reported that he could not take my advances any longer. She knew that was not the way it was and said she could vouch for me and that it was a lie. Anyway, all hell had let loose and they said I was obviously of low moral character but fortunately Marion was able to get it all straightened out. The top brass thought so much of her that she carried the day with her persuasive arguments.

It had obviously been a set up to discredit me and break up my relationship with Army. It failed thank goodness. They then put me up in London at the large Hotel at Marble Arch which was full of American servicemen and women, while I was awaiting another assignment.

The next morning I was walking down Oxford St. when I bumped into Bobbie. We had not seen each other since I had broken up with him a year before I married Andy. He was delighted to see me and insisted we go to a restaurant and talk. He was always good company and I was so pleased that he did not hold any animosity toward me; it was great to be talking with him as a friend again.

He told me he had married and divorced and that he was on an assignment he could not talk about. Knowing his command of Russian and other languages, I was not surprised and being that he was not in uniform I figured he was doing undercover work. The time flew by and as I left him he asked me to have dinner with him that night which I readily agreed to. After that we met for lunch and or dinner every day and I was no longer bored in London.

Then one day he said we seem to have done all the restaurants could he bring a picnic to the Cumberland Hotel and we could have it in my room. I was thrilled as I was tired of going out all the time. He insisted on bringing the food so I provided the wine and we had a wonderful meal. He had put together caviar and smoked salmon and a wonderful repast it turned out to be. We sat on the floor with our wine and all the goodies and talked of old times.

We were laughing so much as we caught up on our lives since the time we had become secretly engaged. When he said he should be leaving, we packed everything up, washed up in the bathroom and I checked the time. It was after nine o'clock at night and I remembered a notice that had been in my room saying that the Hotel had made it a rule that visitors to rooms had to be gone by six o'clock and that someone would be posted at the end of each corridor to enforce this rule.

We had had enough to drink to think it funny or at least he did. I was scared and would not let him leave without my scouting to see if any person was sitting at the end of the corridor. I peeked out of my room and sure enough a man was sitting there. There was nothing for us to do but to have him stay the night and leave early in the morning when the man had gone. He put two chairs together and draped his lanky form over them while I slept fully dressed on the bed. Neither of us were able to sleep very well and early the next morning he said he was leaving and for me not to move saying he had scouted out the passage way. He teased me and was very jolly which annoyed me.

After he left, I settled down and went into a deep sleep to be woken by the phone ringing. I thought right away of Bob calling me to tell me he had made it out, so when I heard a male voice I said "Oh no, Bob, what the hell happened? You only left me an hour ago". There was a long silence and then the phone hung up. A fraction too late, I realized it was Army's voice. He had returned from his assignment no doubt and was getting back in touch.

Now I was in real trouble. How would I ever explain that! Shortly after that a paper was pushed under the door. When I read it I had another fit as it said when I went out to be sure and come to the office. All I could think of was that Bob had been caught and I would be in big trouble with the Red Cross.

I never called Army so I would have to wait for him to call again, if he ever would. When I went out, I got up the courage to go into the office and there they handed me a note which said that Army had called early the day before. I had simply not called in to the desk for any messages. What a mistake. A couple of days went by before Army called again. I knew he did not believe my stupid story even though it happened to be true!

Soon I got my next assignment from the Red Cross which was to take three VIPs on a trip to Devon and Cornwall. They wanted to see all that area of south England before going back to the States and I was considered the best guide since I was British!!

I had never been to that area so I was delighted and studied the Map and called my Mother who had been to Devon and told me of little places such as Truro. Of course it would be difficult driving as being wartime there were no road signs or anything to tell you where you were or where you were going! It was a real challenge as I did not want them to think I was not familiar with the area.

My traveling companions were very nice and soon got over the shock at having a girl driver and guide. I got a little lost outside of Southampton but soon got back on the road and arrived in Devon finding the best Hotel where we settled in.

We had to carry our own luggage and inside we only got the bare necessities. The hotel in those times was operating on a very small staff and the whole place was in darkness with just enough light to find ones way around.

I got directions to the restaurant in the harbor and we went there for dinner. It was just the thing for my companions - a rustic restaurant overlooking the harbor serving shell fish and mainly lobsters. So after an enormous meal of Lobsters we staggered back to the car and the hotel.

On the next day we walked around the village of Truro and then drove on to Land's End which being war time was deserted. We all enjoyed nosing around and being in uniform we were not questioned. We stayed at another small hotel and again had to carry our own luggage.

We returned via Torquay arriving there in the evening. We got out of the car a little exhausted and started lugging our luggage when a boy turned up in the hotel uniform and wrestled our luggage from us.

The lights were all on in the hotel and it was fully staffed and very pre-war. When we registered they asked if we would like breakfast in bed and I was quick to recover and say "yes". The men did not want that but I was tired out and felt I should take advantage of any luxury I could.

The orchestra was playing, people were dancing and dining so we went up to our rooms and freshened up. Then we got together a bit wide eyed for dinner. It was like landing on another planet. We were sad to leave there the next morning. It was I believe the only place that stayed on a pre-war footing all through the war. Torquay was a popular resort but I had never been there before.

We parted company the next day and they returned to the U.S. On my return I checked in to Red Cross H.Q. and was told I should stay in London for a few days.

I got myself a room in Kensington in a boarding house. Army was away again so I knew I would not be seeing him. I went to the Dorchester Hotel with a girl I had met in the Red Cross. We soon had some men around asking us to dance. We had drinks and she left with one of the men.

When I got up to leave, one man said he would like me to have dinner with him. I told him that if I did, he had to understand dinner was not a free ticket to anything else. When we had established that and he still wanted me to dine with him, we went off to dinner.

He was a jolly character in the U.S. forces.

He insisted on seeing me back to my house afterwards and as we said goodnight the air raid warning siren sounded so I of course told him to come in. I had to take him up to my room as there were no lounges or rooms to sit in downstairs.

I offered him a drink and we sat and chatted and laughed. He told me he was a photographer and was aiming at making a career of photography. After several drinks he asked me to pose for him. I was feeling no pain and thought it fun to pose but was really stupid. He kept asking me to pull my skirts up higher and show a lot of leg.

I thought nothing of it until some days later I was told the picture was the pin up for the U.S. forces in the Red Cross clubs! Again trouble and hard to explain to Army! I was young and trusting and very naive.

My next assignment was back with Marion and I was able to get back my little cottage in Amersham. Army joined me in London before I moved and one evening walking back to his hotel, we passed a pet shop where I saw a small furry black thing in the window. It was a Pekinese, the small sleeve type, and I wanted it so badly but the shop was closed. Next day it was delivered to my room and I knew where it came from. I called him Francis. He was all black with a tiny bit of white on the chest and the two front paws. Next day I left for the country with Francis tucked in my battle jacket. He was to see much of the war there!

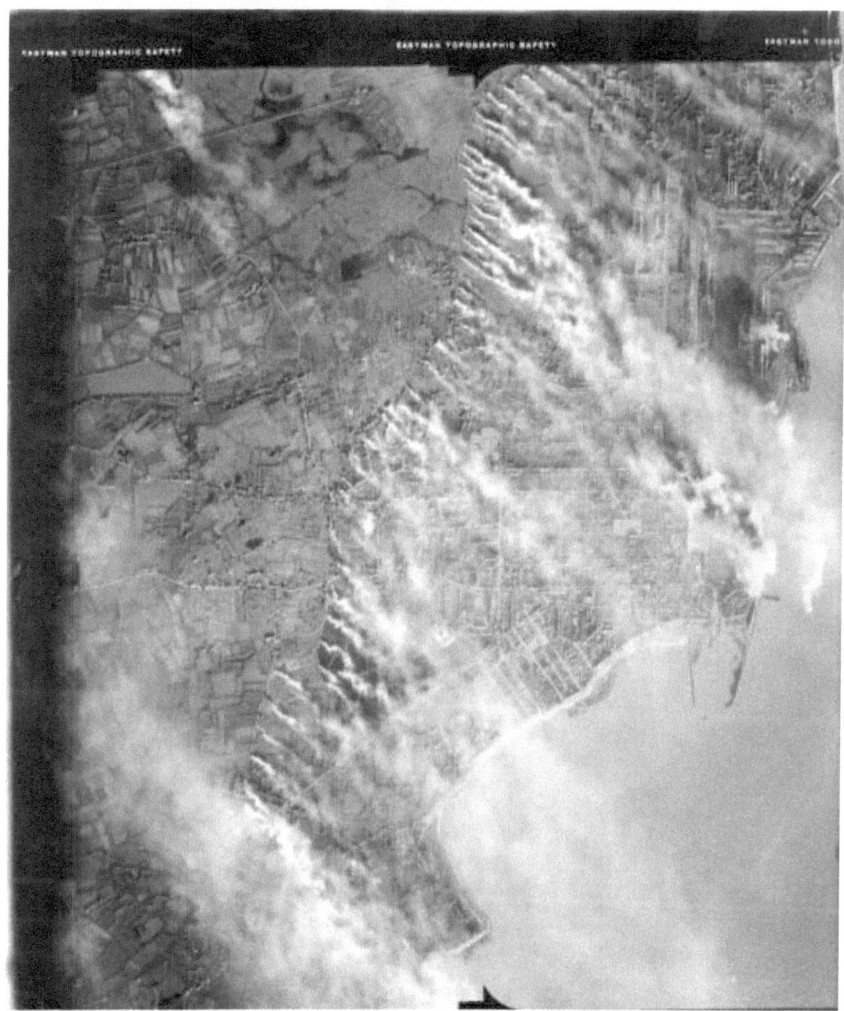

Reconnaissance pictures taken before the run showed the Nazis lighting fires to put up a smokescreen so Allied bombers could not see their targets. This is an original photograph produced by AAF Intelligence.

Aerial reconnaissance played a major role in identifying the B-17G targets. The above original photograph shows the U-Boat base in St. Nazaire, France. Clearly marked are fuel tanks, rail yards and submarine pens to be attacked during the upcoming bombing run.

The first Army Air Force raid over Germany took place on February 27th 1943. A picture of the crew was inscribed by Colonel Armstrong and noted that the Captain died due to enemy action on his next raid on April 16th 1943. The first raid on Germany was over Wilhelmshaven.

Tail gunner Sgt. Love and his twins.

THE STARS AND STRIPES   Monday, Feb. 1, 1943

'Journey's End' for American Bombs on Wilhelmshaven

22 FIGHTERS SHOT DOWN

U.S. BOMBERS' TOLL

United States Flying Fortresses and Liberators destroyed 22 German fighters during their first raid on German territory on Wednesday, it was announced by the U.S. Army Eighth Air Force H.Q. yesterday.

The leading Fortress, which was the first American bomber to fly over German soil, was piloted by Col. Frank A. Armstrong, Junr., one of his most experienced group commanders with the heavy bomber squadrons. A D.F.C. before he came to Britain, he was awarded the silver star for his leadership of the first U.S. heavy bomber raid over Nazi-occupied territory on August 17 last year.

Picture of raid—Page 3

It's "Journey's End" among the lock gates at Wilhelmshaven for bombs dropped by Flying Fortresses of the Eighth Air Force during the first U.S. bombing raid on Germany. Wilhelmshaven is the second most important German naval base for capital ship building, repair and maintenance.

May 22 1943

U.S. Fliers Win British Awards

Twelve Eighth Air Force fliers have been awarded British war decorations by Air Chief Marshal Sir Arthur Tedder of the RAF. They are the first U.S. airmen to receive British decorations for achievements in action with the USAAF.

The awards, nine British DFCs and three DFMs, were presented at a recent "Bomber Night" ceremony at Eighth Air Force Bomber Command Headquarters in the presence of Lt. Gen. Jacob L. Devers, ETO chief, and Maj. Gen. Follett Bradley, inspector general of the USAAF.

Awarded the British DFC were: Brig. Gen. Frank A. Armstrong, Nashville, N.C.; Col. Curtis E. LeMay, Columbus, Ohio; Col. James H. Wallace, Washington; Col. Stanley T. Wray, Birmingham, Ala.; Col. Claude E. Putnam, Jacksboro, Tex.; Maj. Robert B. Keck, Allentown, Pa.; Capt. W. T. Holmes, Denton, Tex.; 1/Lt. George J. Oerider, Dayton, Ohio, and 1/Lt. Anthony C. Venclavage, Kingston, Pa.

The British DFM was awarded to S/Sgt. Conrad Kicklighter, Alma, Ga.; T/Sgt. C. P. Fehr, Madill, Okla., and T/Sgt. J. E. Holl, Dallas, Tex.

Saturday, July 3, 1943

First British Medals to U.S. Airmen

Air Chief Marshal Sir Arthur Harris, chief of RAF bomber command, pins a British DFC on Col. Stanley T. Wray, of Muncie, Ind., as Brig. Gen. Frank Armstrong, an Eighth Air Force wing commander from Rocky Mountain, N.C., looks on during presentation of British DFCs to Eighth U.S. airmen.

U. S. Army Signal Corps Photo

63 British DFCs, and 18 DFMs Awarded Yanks During War

Sixty-three British Distinguished Flying Crosses have been awarded to U.S. fliers since the beginning of the war, the Air Ministry revealed yesterday. Fifty-four of these were given to Americans serving with the RAF and RCAF, and nine were awarded recently to Eighth Air Force officers when the RAF broke a long-standing tradition and honored American group commanders and individual heroes with the British DFC.

Lt. General Jacob Devers was the Commander of US Army Forces Europe and personally came to congratulate the 8th Bomber Group together with Sir Anthony Eden who at the time was the Foreign Secretary and would later become Prime Minister in the 1950s.

Along with Brigadier General Eaker is Brigadier General Samuel E. Anderson who was Commander of the 9th Bomber Group.

Here members of the 8th Bomber Group receive accolades and awards after flying 25 Missions over Europe.

1943

Fortresses

shot down 22 over Germany
Anglo-American forces keep up raid 'umbrella' for a month

TWENTY-TWO German fighters were destroyed by the U.S. Flying Fortresses and Liberators which carried out their first bombing of German territory last Wednesday. This was announced last night by the headquarters of the U.S. Army Eighth Air Force.

This total, it was added, had been fixed after a complete sifting of claims. Three U.S. bombers were lost in the operation.

It was also announced last night the bombing Fortress on Wednesday's raid, piloted by Colonel Frank A. Armstrong Jun., was first over German soil.

Round-the-clock

Because bombs were dropped at more than one point in Germany it was explained, it probably would be impossible to answer officially persistent inquiries about which bombers' crew, or bombardier, was first to drop explosives.

This month the R.A.F. and U.S. Air Forces in Britain have almost maintained a "24-hours-a-day umbrella" over the Continent.

General saved his navigator

The D.S.C.—second highest U.S. gallantry award—has been given to Brig.-General Frank A. Armstrong who, after his plane had fought off 35 German fighters, left the controls to give first aid to the wounded navigator, saving his life.

It was on April 5. General Armstrong was leading U.S. bombers raiding Antwerp. They were attacked by 100 German fighters. Yet they successfully finished their job.

General Armstrong is 41. Once he was a professional baseball player. Since then he has led the first U.S. day raid on Germany.

Marion and I resumed much of the same work as before and by then Army was in command of a Wing. So I saw a lot of him there or at my cottage but he would never arrive without an invitation. He always had his driver park way down the street so as not to cause me any embarrassment.

He loved my little dog but always kidded me about him and never admitted to giving him to me. Francis traveled with me to the air bases

every day and when we got to one he would jump out of the car and head for the kitchens. How he knew I never could make out but that is where he would go and the men would make such a fuss of him. I presume it was his nose that told him where to go! So when I came out of a meeting there Francis would be sitting on top of a jeep and the men just standing around petting him.

One day he was on top of a truck and decided he could fly and took a leap off and of course broke his leg. He did not try to fly again. Army was amused that I would call that little ball of fluff after him. He would always chuckle about it. All the air bases knew Francis. He was such a character and his little face would peek out of my battle jacket when the weather was wet or cold.

We were still living day to day as one did not know what the next day would bring or if one would be around to even see it.

It was a sad time but also one enjoyed the few days one did have and appreciated every moment one was allowed to have together. Sometimes Army came with me to my parent's estate in Maidenhead along with Francis and some friends to enjoy a few days of peace.

One day, while walking back to my cottage from a pub we had been to, we passed a Carousel packing up for the night. I jumped on it and dragged Army with me and we rode the horses around and around.

It was quite crazy and so much fun though of course hardly the place for a General!! At the Pub there had been a Wishing Well and I insisted on making a wish, a wish I never thought could come true.

We knew our time together was running out. We did not talk about it but the knowledge was always there.

Then one day he just could not leave. We clung to each other and although he had not said anything I sensed this was it. We had discussed our relationship early on and he had felt it was not fair to tie me to him when he moved on to the Japanese Theater.

He felt I would go back to my husband when all this was over. I felt he was wrong about that. Nothing would make me go back to Andy once I had known real love. However, it was better for us both to remember this as a beautiful war time romance and not to try to find each other again. He finally tore himself away and strode out. I cried most of the next day and Marion knew without asking what had happened.

Late the next day he called, his orders were changed and we had a few more days together. Again the day came and for a strong man he was so incredibly gentle. I knew this was it and there would not be another reprieve.

When he left in the early hours of the morning, he said: "do not move Honey. Let me remember you there."

He turned on his heels and was gone.

That day I knew it was final and I did not leave the bed all day, my voice said it all when I called Marion and she was very understanding. I felt my world had come to an end. I cuddled Francis who seemed to know too. All I had were his little notes to console myself.

Every day seemed empty to me with Army gone out of it. There seemed no sense to anything I did and I grew very depressed.

Our work at the Bases had come to an end and I was finally given another assignment which was to report to a rehabilitation center for officers before they returned to active duty.

'Forts' Smash at Antwerp

APRIL 5ᵉ
1943

ANTWERP AERO WORKS GUTTED

THE main building of the Erla aero-engine works was completely gutted during Monday's daylight raid on Antwerp by Flying Fortresses and Liberators, the H.Q. of U.S. European Theatre of Operations announced last night.

The Erla works is an important repair depot for single-engined German fighters. In peace-time the plant manufactured Minerva automobiles.

The Gevaert Photographic Producta plant, near the Erla works, was also badly hit and the main building was fired.

A single group of Fortresses took the brunt of the attacks by swarms of Nazi fighters, which dived on them from all directions, sometimes three abreast.

Brigadier-General Frank Armstrong flew as an observer to this group.

The Luftwaffe defences in Western Europe were again spreadeagled yesterday. A strong force of Flying Fortresses and Liberators followed the previous night's R.A.F. raid on Kiel by bombing the Erla Aero Engine Works at Antwerp.

And while the Americans were making their first raid on the Belgian port, Venturas of Bomber Command smashed at Brest docks and shipping.

Allied losses were light; four bombers and one fighter at Antwerp, three bombers and a fighter over Brest.

Two German fighters were claimed as destroyed in the Belgian raid, one at Brest. These figures do not include victories by the American bombers, since their results have not yet been assessed.

It was the American Air Force's first attack on Antwerp. Visibility was good, and results satisfactory. The flak was hundreds feet accurate.

The German fighters appeared to be adopting new tactics by concentrating chiefly on one group of bombers.

Pilots of this force reported the opposition was the fiercest they had ever known. Others point out they met with comparatively little trouble.

As the bombers approached the coast Focke-Wulf 190s and Messerschmitt 109s met them. They followed on to the target and then chased the Americans out to sea again.

50 FIGHTERS

Some of the bomber crews took part in Sunday's raid on the Renault works at Paris.

One of them said: "I think the bombing was good, but I couldn't observe it as well as that at the Renault factory yesterday."

About 50 enemy fighters hovered above the bombers but did not attack. They seemed to be looking for stragglers.

One Fortress tried over the target was hit by flak and fighters at the same time.

Both port engines were damaged. The oxygen system was hit, control cables were broken, and the pilot had to leave the formation through lack of oxygen and head for home escorted by a Spitfire.

Armbishop Spellman, accompanied by Brig.-Gen. Newton Longfellow, Commanding General, American Bomber Command, visited several airfields before the raid.

A number of Catholic airmen received Holy Communion and the Papal Blessing from the Archbishop.

He then shook hands with the men and promised to write to their families if they left names and addresses with their station chaplains.

GENERAL SAVES HIS MAN

BRIGADIER - GENERAL FRANK A. ARMSTRONG, who led the first all-American attack over German-occupied territory last year, saved the life of a badly wounded navigator after their Flying Fortress had been hit by a shell when raiding Antwerp on Monday. It was revealed last night.

General Armstrong, flying in the raid as observer, acting as interior to the plane when it was attacked by a large number of German fighters in what is described as the most intense battle yet.

A 20 mm. shell crashed through the plane nose, seriously wounding the navigator, putting out of action the instrument and oxygen systems and damaging a propeller.

Lack of oxygen

General Armstrong grabbed an oxygen bottle and went to the help of the navigator, who was apparently dying. He was bleeding profusely from a cut.

He helped ease the general himself that he flew applied the instruments to her own hand.

Later, when he landed, he was still suffering from lack of oxygen in such an extent that he could not remember the name of his pilot.

Yesterday the navigator was reported as recovering in a hospital with the aid of blood transfusions.

In 1949 this story about the 8th Air Force was published and then became a hit movie. General Frank Savage was largely based on Frank Armstrong and the exploits of his bomber group formed the backdrop. The character Pamela was also loosely based on Boo-Boo.

Sy Bartlett was in Group Operations while Beirne Lay was a pilot and veteran of many missions.

Frank Armstrong put together scrapbooks during his entire career. After his death, they were given to the J. Y. Joyner Library at the East Carolina University.

However, his scrap book about the 1942 to 1944 period in England he gave to Boo-Boo.

It had 30 pages of photos and clippings including a handwritten epitaph at the end.

It read as follows:

"Boo! Honey–

In the back pages of your book and more than likely the back pages of your life, I take this rare opportunity of expressing my thoughts – if one could call them thoughts.

Since my arrival in England, the second time, you and "the Cheshams" have done all that any persons could do to add sunshine and hope and happiness to one person's life – and existence. Mostly you "young lady" have cemented the friendship of the "allied nations" so far as I am concerned. I am sorry that I could not have done more towards winning the war. My efforts were feeble compared to others. However, in the days to come you may rest assured that your influence upon me will have done much to have governed the tract of my mind – my affections – my devotions and my sincere love for you and those who saw the Americans through the "rough spots" –

The least I can say is: My love to you –

Frank Armstrong
POST-WAR

Armstrong continued his Air Force career following World War II, first becoming chief of staff for operations of the Pacific Air Command on January 18, 1946, and then senior air advisor at the Armed Forces Staff College, Norfolk, Virginia, on September 9, 1946. After creation of the United States Air Force, Gen. Armstrong served as deputy commanding general of the Alaskan Air Command at Fort Richardson, Alaska (March 31, 1948), and its commanding general (February 26, 1949, to December 26, 1950). While commander, he was awarded the Gold Medal of the Aero Club of Norway, the highest civil award of Norway, for helping develop a non-stop polar air route from Alaska to Norway to New York.

10 years later….. 1954

The divorce from Andy was nearly final. The boys were in school in Geneva so I went over to England and stayed at the family home with my brother Derek and his wife Maggie who had settled in the country house in Maidenhead. That evening we were talking and Maggie said to me:

"Oh, Mary, I was at a cocktail party last week and met a friend of yours who thought you were dead. Apparently, he knew you during the war. He is an American author and he made me promise that I would have you call him when you arrived. Here is his number."

I said that I would not call him and I knew who he was. I did not want to stir up old memories. The connection of course was that he was the author of "Twelve O'clock High", the book about Army and the Eighth Bomber Group. I of course figured in it under another name. Maggie would not take a simple no. She said she had promised him that I would call. So just before returning to Switzerland I was in London and I gave Sy Bartlett a call.

He was so pleased and asked me to go around and have a drink with him. I declined but after a while he persuaded me to go. We had a great reunion and he told me how he had been with Army when someone just back from London told them that there had been the announcement of my death in the paper. They had a drink and toasted me and reminded each other of all the good times we had together during the war.

He said that Army had been so very upset by the news of my death. Sy then asked me to please get in touch with Army and gave me his address. I told him I didn't want to and that it was history and lovely while it lasted but that was ten years ago.

Well he did not give up and begged me to at least write to him. Finally, I said I would send him a Christmas card as it was just a couple of weeks before Xmas.

I went back to Geneva and I did send a card just saying "Ha, I am still alive, best wishes." I really wondered if I would hear anything back.

Almost by return mail, I had a long letter from Army who was very pleased to know I was alive and said he would be in London on the 13th of January and asked if I could meet him there?

It so happened that my lawyer had given me that date to sign papers for the release of my assets. The very date seemed like fate and therefore I should go along with it.

I was very nervous about seeing him again after 10 years. Would we wonder what on earth we had seen in each other? Was it a big mistake to spoil something that had been so wonderful while I was so young and there had been a war raging all around us? He was almost twenty years older than I was. Well it did seem fateful and I did not believe in going against fate. So I wrote back telling him just that and that he should call me when he got to London. I would be staying with an old friend in the city. He wrote back very quickly telling me how happy he was and that I should figure on having dinner with him that night.

I arrived in London at Bette's apartment around 4 pm and Bette made a cup of tea. We chatted away catching up on each other's news. We had not seen each other for some time due to my living abroad so much and we had not seen each other during the war at all so she did not know of my affair with an American.

She was curious as to whom I was dining with and I had to tell her the whole story and the nervousness I was feeling at meeting him again after so much time. I changed into a navy blue silk cocktail dress and saw that my figure was still good which gave me some confidence.

The bell rang and Bette told me to go down to the hall to meet him as she pressed the button opening the front door.

I reached the bottom of the stairs as the door swung open, I think my heart stopped, certainly time stood still as he walked in. Then I was back in real time – nothing had changed and we were in each other's arms.

He had not changed.

We went up and joined Bette for a drink. It was the most amazing thing here we were and the ten years we had not been in touch faded away.

He took me out to dinner and told me that he had always loved me and how devastated he had been on hearing that I had died.

We figured it out that someone had seen the notice of my mother's death and since I went under the name of Hall Caine in the service and no one knew my first name as Army had named me Bo-Boo and everyone knew me as Boo.

I had asked him never to say he loved me. I think partly because I had been so disillusioned and partly I felt if we never said we loved each other it would never be hard to separate. What a mistake that was!

The next night he was very mysterious as he took me to eat early and then we went on where there were a lot of Air Corps gathered. He settled me in a seat and then went up on the stage. There were all kinds of Brass there who all spoke glowingly of him

He spoke and to my shock said he could never have achieved the things he did and the rank had it not been for a young lady and then he introduced me and I rushed onto the stage to much applause. I had been with him for each promotion and it was really extraordinary that we were reunited just in time for this.

He was so happy.

Another thing that made him happy was to learn that I was about to go to the U.S. and settle in Washington D.C. He told me although he was stationed in Alaska he had to go to Washington frequently so we would be able to see a lot of each other.

He was in fact Commander in Chief of the combined Alaskan Military Command. We had a wonderful few days together before he left to return to the US and I went back to Switzerland and resumed packing up and making final arrangements for my departure to Washington DC in the USA.

Frank standing in front of a B-47B Stratojet of the 306th Bomb Wing (Medium) at MacDill AFB, Florida.

On January 13, 1950, Armstrong was promoted to major general and named base commander of Sampson Air Force Base, New York, in January 1951. On May 13, 1951, he became commanding general of the Sixth Air Division, training the first B-47 Stratojet Wing at MacDill Air Force Base, Florida, and in 1952, commander of the Second Air Force (Strategic Air Command) at Barksdale Air Force Base, a post he held for four years.

5 years later 1955

After moving in to our first house on Glover Driveway in Washington's fashionable northwest area, we went through our first hurricane. Hurricane Hazel proved to be quite an experience. I thought the car would be swept away – the rain was torrential. We had done as told and stocked up on food and water but it luckily did not turn out to be as bad as previously expected.

Frank (Army) arrived soon after and he and his aide, Major George Dalferes, came to the house to meet the boys and their nanny who he called

*my "girl Friday". We had drinks on the screened terrace and then Frank,
George and I went out to dinner. That was about the way my life went
for the next three years. The three of us were always together in public.*

*After a couple of months I moved to Upton Street just off Reno Road
and Frank would come and play ping pong with Nicki. Once, General
James Doolittle, another wartime friend came by and took Nicki and me
to see a war film called "Bridge over the River Kwai". George would
usually come to the house to pick me up and I am sure most people thought
he was my boyfriend! That was fine with me as he was not married and
of course much nearer my age.*

Frank's final posting was in July 1956, again as head of the
Alaskan Air Command, and upon his promotion to lieutenant
general, as commander of the Joint Alaskan Military Command.

Shortly afterwards, the newly minted Lieutenant General visited
allies in the Pacific Rim countries including Thailand. There he
presented a special award: The Eternal Spirit of the Arctic Empire
to Fuen Ronnaphagrad Ritthakhanee who was by then a marshal
of the Royal Thai Air Force and its Commander.

3 years later...... 1958

After arriving in Washington, DC I was reacquainted with a man, Courtney Burr, who I had met in Austria before the war. I told him about Frank.

Courtney was getting very serious about me and asked me to marry him. He said he was an Investment Banker in N.Y. so it would mean my moving up there. We talked everything over but I said I could not give him an answer.

That next week I gave it a lot of serious thought. It made sense for me to marry him. I could not imagine anyone else who came near to someone I could live with but the fact remained that I was not in love with him and I was in love with Frank! What to do?

I really did need to settle down and have a father figure for the boys. I did like him immensely and as a friend he was perfect but was it fair to marry him under those conditions?

Frank and I had talked of marriage but I knew I could never be the wife of a military man. Also he was a man's man. He had been a professional baseball player in his early years and I knew nothing of baseball – in fact it bored me. The Air Force meant everything to him but it was not my life. We had little in common. During the war it was alright but now it was something else. We really had come from two different worlds.

Courtney brought his son down to Washington and Nicki and the younger Courtney really enjoyed being together. Nicki was just one year older. Courtney wanted my answer and I told him that I had to see Frank because we had agreed never to just walk out on each other.

Courtney told me he was on his way to California to see his mother and that I should give him my answer on his return. Time was not on my side as if I was to marry him and move to N.Y. area there was little time to enroll the boys in school as it was already August.

Frank was due to come the next week. I unfortunately became ill and it seemed like Mumps. The doctor prescribed medication and ordered me to stay in bed. Frank called me upon reaching Washington and I had to tell him that I was ill with the Mumps.

He of course said he could not come near me which I understood. I told him I wanted to talk to him and he said he would be coming back in a couple of weeks because he was headed south to Puerto Rico and we could talk then.

As fate would have it he did not come back but instead went straight back to Alaska. There was no way I could talk to him on the phone about such a delicate matter and I would not even try. I owed it to him to talk face to face and explain my intentions. I waited but time was running out.

Courtney had come to see me while I had Mumps and it had not bothered him. Of course, Frank knew nothing of Courtney.

I had to do a lot of soul searching. I had loved Frank, even worshiped him when I was very young through the hard war years and had stayed in love with him even though I went back to Andy after the war and never expected to see Frank again.

But after ten years, fate brings us together again It was meant to be but I was not happy with the way it was. We had to be so discreet and hiding out was not a way I wanted to live. My being in D.C. and him so far away on the other side of the United States, visiting once a month if we were lucky, was really not satisfactory.

I needed a man to help me with the boys and my life in general. I did go out with other men and he accepted that but I knew he was jealous and it was not easy for either of us. If I had not had children, I would have moved to Alaska or at any rate closer so that we could have had the relationship we had during the war. Yet we had so little in common. If we had married I knew it would never work for him any more than it would for me. I was not getting any younger and neither was he. How long would we keep up this way of living?

I also accepted the fact that I needed to settle down and make a well-rounded home for my boys and Courtney coming back into my life at this very time was again fate! It was meant to be. He was ideal. I liked him very much. He had mixed with many of my friends in England and he came from much the same background as I did. Educated in Europe, he spoke French, enjoyed Tennis, Skiing, and Skating etc. He had fallen for me the short time we were in Austria together when I was just 19. It all made sense. He was nice looking, a good dancer and what more did I want or expect to find? The likelihood of my meeting and falling in love again with someone who had all these attributes was 100 to 1.

So as hard as it was, and it was very hard, I steeled myself and made the decision to accept his proposal.

I had no intention of getting married until I had seen Frank and told him in person of my decision but time was getting short and I knew I had to sell the house and move to N.Y. State so as to settle the boys in school in time for the coming year.

Frank kept saying he would be in Washington very soon but his orders were always changing and he did not come. After I had met Courtney again, it was clear he was very interested in me. I saw the possibility of marrying him and wondered what I would do if he were to actually ask me? So when Frank finally got to Washington, I told Frank that I was thinking I should settle down and find a man I could marry. He laughed and said," Honey you will never leave me". For a moment I thought he may just be right: I never could leave him. Yet here I was in fact thinking of doing just that.

Frank did not come back and Courtney of course proposed marriage and wanted an answer. He was getting a little impatient and so I agreed to marry him as I knew it was the right thing for the boys and I would never find someone I cared for more as a friend than Courtney.

I had been honest with him and told him I did not love him. He accepted that and said he was not worried on that score and said in time I would grow to love him.

GEN. F. A. ARMSTRONG

Gen. Armstrong Wins Promotion

The United States Air Force announced in Washington yesterday that President Eisenhower has confirmed the promotion to lieutenant-general for Frank A. Armstrong Jr., commander-in-chief of the Alaskan Command.

The third star for the former Second Air Force commander became effective Monday. Gen. Armstrong served as commander of the Second Air Force, with headquarters at Barksdale Air Force Base, from 1952 until last July, when he turned over his command here to Maj. Gen. George W. Mundy.

From Barksdale, he traveled to Alaska to take his new assignment of commander for the Alaskan Air Command, from which he was named to the commander-in-chief position for the entire Alaskan Command.

General Armstrong commanded the first B47 Stratojet wing in the Air Force, and during his command at Barksdale, converted the Second Air Force into the first all-jet Air Force.

1 year later 1959

Then I got a letter from Frank. He was terribly distressed. He had gone to Washington only to find that my phone number was discontinued. He drove around to the house and found it empty and up for sale!! He could not imagine what had happened and asked me to please contact him as soon as I possibly could.

So I had to write the letter I had never wanted to write. In the letter he wrote back to me, he was very understanding and said he knew I had done the right thing but that his love for me would always be the same.

I never saw him again.

Monday 2.

Dear Jan:

I have been worried about your where-abouts. Thanks for letting me know that you are well & happy.

Your Choice was excellent and I wish you two all the happiness in the whole world.

Dawn & Jean. San Francisco was chosen by a rather keen Jake. We are in the midst of the worse snow storm in years. We have evacuated the headquarters building and requested [army] tanks stand by to keep stalled cars. Geo. Oljeyere will be married in April. I am to be best man. I am on a trip Japan, Hawaii and as far south as Puerto Rico. Now you know. End news.

I have no idea where I will go from Alaska or whither I will continue for another year. April or may should bring forth the answer. I have had a very fine offer from a world wide construction company. I may stay on until Senator Symington is elected President. I may go fishing. Come what may I am in no hurry to map out any future plans. One thing certain. I do not want the Pentagon.

Monday 2. (March 1959)

"Dear Mary,

I have been worried about your whereabouts. Thanks for letting me know that you are well and happy.

Your choice was excellent and I wish you two all the happiness in the whole world.

News Flash, San Francisco was shaken by a rather heavy shake. We are in the midst of the worst snow storm in years. We have evacuated the headquarters building and requested Army tanks standby to help stalled cars. George Dalferes will be married in April. I am to be best man. I was on a trip to Japan. Hawaii and as far south as Puerto Rico. Now you know. End News.

I have no idea where I will go from Alaska or whether I will continue for another year. April or May should bring forth the answer. I have had a very good offer from a worldwide construction company. I may stay on until Senator Symington is elected President. I may go fishing. Come what may I am in no hurry to map out any future plans. One thing certain, I do not want the Pentagon."

It is nice that your boys are doing well (my ping pong is better).

At the time I want you to know that you were wonderful to me – most of the time. In England your presence was a great morale builder. Raids were longer – especially the early ones.

I hear from General Raymond once in a while. I shall pass your regards on to him when I see him.

I have not been to Washington since I spoke with you however I am to attend a briefing in April. Must remind myself not to call Upton.

This is not a letter – just rambling along

Thanks again for letting me know that you are safe and sound.

Give my best to your girl "Friday".

For you – everything that is good for you.

No change.

Frank

He sent his Aide, Major George Dalferes, who I knew well to visit me every few months to see if I was happy and alright. We would talk of Frank and I would tell George to tell Frank I felt the same about him and always would.

He would come to the house but never stayed long.

George Dalferes was born Feb. 25, 1923, in Warsaw, Poland, to Sabin Jean Dalferes and Jadwiga Drzewinska Dalferes. He died September 8th, 2006. A veteran of the 84th Infantry Division in World War II, he was mobilized again in 1952 for the Korean War and served in the U.S. Air Force as an aide for many years to Lt. Gen. Frank Armstrong, commander of the Alaskan Command. During his second tour of duty at Elmendorf Air Force Base, he met his future wife, Georgie Evelyn Boling, an Air Force captain and nurse stationed in Fairbanks. After their 1959 marriage, the couple deployed on various tours of duty, finally settling in Washington, D.C., where he served as deputy assistant to the secretary of defense for legislative affairs at the Pentagon.

Upon retiring from the military, Col. Dalferes represented the aerospace division of the Martin Marietta Corp. in the nation's capital for 17 years as vice president of government affairs. He retired in 1990. He then consulted for the aerospace industry and NASA and served as legislative counsel for former President George H.W.

Bush's 1990 Stafford Commission, which examined the country's long-term goals for space.

I often wondered if Frank had made it to Washington and I had told him in person if I would have ever been able to leave him. I knew then that it was good that fate had stepped in to make it impossible for me to see him and tell him face to face what I was going to do. If I had I would probably never have had the courage to leave him. Over the next years he sent his aide, George to visit me and make sure I was happy and well cared for. Every year George would call and ask if he could come by and see me, he would leave reassured that all was well.

Then he traced me when we moved to Connecticut in 1963 and called me there after Frank had retired. He was still checking on me.

In 1966 my son Nicki joined the Air Force to avoid being drafted into the Army. I was mortified. In the summer of 1967 he was assigned some duties in North Carolina and contacted Frank. He said they had a great visit together. A few months later we learned that Frank's son had been shot down in Vietnam.

Frank died two years later in August of 1969 and I received one call from George asking me if I knew.

I never saw nor heard from George again.

Epilogue

In the end, Boo-Boo and the General finished their days in obscurity and apart. As General MacArthur so aptly said: "they just quietly faded away" as all good soldiers do.

The General retired in 1962 and died 7 years later on August 20th, 1969. He was buried along with other heroes in the Arlington National Cemetery, SECTION 34 SITE 13-A. Sadly, the remains of his own son who had been killed in action over Vietnam barely two years earlier were never recovered.

He helped usher in the jet age and lived long enough to see another Colonel with his surname set foot on the moon.

Boo-Boo buried her second husband, Courtney, in 1994 and moved to Stuart, Florida. She was active as the Secretary of the Daughters of the British Empire chapter in Stuart and visited the 8th Air Force Museum in Savannah, Georgia. Her son, Nicholas, moved to Palm City to be closer to her in her last year. She planned to visit Frank's gravesite in Washington and even travelled to the library at East Carolina University. She passed away quietly on the 11th of December 2003.

May they both rest in peace and find in eternity
the happiness they had only a brief moment to
enjoy while walking among us here on earth.

"Never in the field of human
conflict was so much owed
by so many to so few."

Winston S. Churchill – 16 August 1940

About the Author

Nicholas Mouravieff-Apostol was born in London, England in 1947, the youngest son of Mary Hall Caine (Boo-Boo) and attended St. Paul's School in Concord, NH and St. Luke's School in New Canaan, Ct. He continued his undergraduate studies in Political Science at the University of Nebraska and did follow-on courses in Business Administration at the City College of Chicago. He served in the US Air Force during the Vietnam conflict earning several awards including a Commendation Medal for Meritorious Service. As an entrepreneur he was an early pioneer in personal computing and the development of the handheld calculator. Later, he was recognized for being an early developer of the Commuter Airline industry and more recently founded several companies and a Foundation which made significant contributions to the recycling of waste plastics and vehicle tires. During the mid-eighties, he went to El Salvador for the Arthur Young accounting firm and headed up numerous development projects. He later served USAID in developing and controlling the billion dollar cash transfer programs which would later be adopted as a model for worldwide use. In 1986, at the request of then President Duarte, he organized the recovery operation following the devastating earthquake. During the final few years of the war there, he served as senior executive advisor to the President in coordinating the peace initiatives. One of his proudest achievements was a program he founded to help those who lost limbs from landmines. Today he lives in Florida with his wife, the former Jeannette Byington on their ranch where she operates a Foundation dedicated to rescuing Macaws. This multilingual, Renaissance man is a licensed commercial pilot, and has published many newspaper articles, a number of poems and several books. Currently, he is writing about his very distinctive paternal as well as maternal family history and an autobiography.

Other publications by the same author

For Better ~ For Worse
> The life of Vladimir Mouravieff-Apostol-Korobyine, a Czarist Russian diplomat (1864- 1937)

The Collected Works of Mary Cicely Hall Caine
> The illustrated guide to the equine paintings of Mary Hall Caine (1925 – 1992)

Through A Lens with Love
> Collection of photographs by Nicholas Apostol (1962-2009)

Mary Hall Caine – Images of a Lifetime
> Illustrated biography of Mary Hall Caine (1917-2003)

El Salvador – Ten Years On (1979-1989)
> Eyewitness account of the civil war with emphasis on the final assault by the FMLN in 1989.

Colours of the Heart
> Collection of Poems

Cottages to Castles
> Illustrated guide to homes and properties owned by the family of Nicholas Mouravieff-Apostol since the 1300s

Yardley Farms
> Illustrated guide to the Apostol farm in Florida

Hacienda Apostol
> Illustrated guide to the Apostol mansion in Puerto Rico

Illustrated Guide to the Writings of Hall Caine
> Illustrated guide to over 400 books, manuscripts, articles and prints of the Manx author Thomas Henry Hall Caine (1851-1931)

Also: Green Hotel Program Guide, Plastic Waste Alternatives, Economic Support Fund Management Guide, COMFIEN 1988-1989, Forever Friends, Animal Welfare and Puerto Rico

www.ingramcontent.com/pod-product-compliance
Lightning Source LLC
Chambersburg PA
CBHW031231120626
46545CB00003B/1078